904000

jB
RAFFI

Spies, Karen
Raffi

jB
RAFFI

Spies, Karen
Raffi

904000

$10.95

The Children's Voice

Karen Spies

Taking part BOOKS

dP DILLON PRESS, INC.
Minneapolis, Minnesota 55415

J B
RAFFI

Photographic Acknowledgments

The photographs have been reproduced through the courtesy of Cavouk (pp. 9, 11, 13, 20, 58), Patrick Harbron (p. 6), John Evans Photo Ltd. (p. 48), Erica King (p. 50), Susan McCord (p. 30), Bert Simpson (pp. 22, 45), and David Street (pp. 35, 38). Cover photo by David Street.

Library of Congress Cataloging-in-Publication Data

Spies, Karen Bornemann.
Raffi : the children's voice / by Karen Spies.
(Taking part)
Includes index.
Summary: Presents the life and career of the popular Canadian performer, discussing his albums, concerts, and latest projects.
ISBN 0-87518-398-0

1. Raffi. 2. Singers—Canada—Biography. [1. Raffi. 2. Singers.] I. Title.
ML3930.R23S6   1989
784.6'24'00924—dc 19
[B]
[92]   88-20298
                                                                  CIP
                                                               AC MN

© 1989 by Dillon Press, Inc. All rights reserved

Dillon Press, Inc., 242 Portland Avenue South
Minneapolis, Minnesota 55415

Printed in the United States of America
1 2 3 4 5 6 7 8 9 10 98 97 96 95 94 93 92 91 90 89

Contents

For Karsten and Astrid

Acknowledgments

My deepest appreciation to Raffi, Debi Pike, and Bert and Bonnie Simpson for their encouragement, support, and assistance in the creation of this book. A special thanks to the entire staff of Troubadour Records Limited for their cooperation and help. My gratitude to Eda LeShan, Catherine Ambrose, Mark Jaffe of A&M Records, and Susan Stewart and Heidi Robinson of Jensen Communications for their willing assistance on this project.

I would also like to thank Troubadour Records Limited for permission to quote from the following songs: "Time to Sing," words and music by Raffi, D. Pike, B. and B. Simpson; © 1985 Homeland Publishing, a division of Troubadour Records Ltd. All rights reserved. "One Light, One Sun," words and music by Raffi; © 1985 Homeland Publishing, a division of Troubadour Records Ltd. All rights reserved.

Raffi

A love of life, children, and music have helped make Canadian singer and guitarist Raffi the most popular children's performer in North America today. Raffi began his singing career in the late 1960s, performing folk music for adult audiences. His earliest performances for children were at nursery schools and libraries in Toronto, Ontario. In 1976, Raffi recorded his first album, *Singable Songs for the Very Young*. It has sold more than 700,000 copies and remains his best-selling record.

Since then, Raffi has recorded seven more highly acclaimed albums and created *Raffi Songs to Read*™, picture books based on his well-known songs. He has also filmed two concert videos. His work has won many awards, including a Grammy nomination for the best children's recording of 1988.

In his songs, Raffi makes use of many musical styles, such as folk, ragtime, and calypso. Parents and teachers especially like the way he sings about love in the family and taking care of the earth. Through his music, Raffi shares his love for all the people and living things in the world. As he says, "I'm here to make music. . .that makes people feel good and brings them together."

1

"Sing When the Spirit Says Sing"

Children press their noses against the glass auditorium doors, waiting for their turn to go inside. Some enter singing. Some skip down the aisle. Others hold tightly to their mom or dad's hand, watching as families fill the auditorium.

Then a bearded man walks on stage. His soft brown eyes twinkling, he calls, "Hi, boys and girls."

Children pop up in their seats. "Hi, Raffi!" they answer back.

Strumming his guitar, he sings, "It's time to sing a song or two. You with me and me with you." Already, the audience has joined in. When the song says, "It's time for us to clap our hands" or "tap our toes," they can't help clapping and tapping.

Everyone is laughing and smiling as they sing along, and this is just what Raffi loves. "When a family comes to a concert together, they sing together. It's a shared activity," he explains.

Since 1978, Raffi has devoted his career to bringing the joy of music to children and their families. Although Raffi has won the applause of both children and adults, he is more concerned with offering good music than with winning awards. He shares his joy of living each time he sings, "You've got to sing when the spirit says sing."

Raffi's deep love for the world around him grew from a family background with roots in several countries. Raffi was born in Cairo, Egypt, on July 8, 1948, to Armenian parents. Armenia was once an independent country in western Asia. Raffi's family was originally from an area that became part of Turkey.

During World War I, Ohannes Cavoukian, Raf-

Six-month-old Raffi.

fi's grandfather, decided to find a safer place for his family to live. Raffi's father Artin was a young boy when the family left Turkey. They stayed in Jerusalem for a few years and then settled on the Mediterranean island of Cyprus. At the end of World War II, the family moved again, this time to Cairo, Egypt.

There Raffi's grandfather opened a portrait photography studio.

By this time, Artin was a grown man, with a family of his own. He and his wife Lucy had three children: Raffi, his older brother Onnig, and his younger sister Ann.

Artin worked with his father at the Cavouk Studio. He thought he would have many years to learn how to take and develop portrait photographs. But in 1952, Raffi's grandfather was hit and killed by a motorcycle as he crossed the street.

Suddenly, Raffi's father was in charge of the busy studio. He worked hard to learn new methods of photography, such as the use of color film. Artin felt portrait photographs would look more lifelike if done in color, so he invented an easier and cheaper way to develop color photos. In the past, photographers had to send color film to large photo labs for

Above: *Raffi (left)* and his brother Onnig with their grandfather
Ohannes Cavoukian. Right: *Raffi's family; (from left to right)*
Lucy, Ann, Onnig, Raffi, and Artin.

developing. Because of Artin's new process, they could at last print and develop their own color pictures.

His father's leadership in the photography business set a good example for Raffi. He learned the importance of hard work. He also began to appreciate many different kinds of people, since people from all over the world came to the Cavouk Studio.

Inside and outside the studio, Raffi heard a number of languages spoken in Cairo, a busy international city. He went to an Armenian private school, where lessons were taught in Armenian except for foreign language classes. There Raffi studied and spoke Arabic, the Egyptian language.

When Raffi was ten, his family left Egypt. His parents believed that Canada offered more freedom to raise a family and operate a business. They settled in Toronto, the capital of the province of Ontario

Young Raffi assists at a display at the Cavouk Studio.

and a bustling port city on Lake Ontario. Business and government leaders from many nations visited Toronto, which made it an ideal location for the Cavouk Studio.

As the business continued to grow, the entire family helped out more. Raffi, Ann, and Onnig helped with cleanup jobs and at photography displays. Artin counted on Lucy's help in many ways, including scheduling appointments. Her friendly manner helped bring business to the Cavouk Studio.

Raffi had to make many adjustments because of the move to Canada. Since he couldn't speak English, no one at the elementary school knew how smart he really was. He was placed in a class with children who were a year younger, and he had to repeat a grade.

Although this setback disappointed Raffi, he soon grew to like his new school. He felt that the Canadian teachers were more caring than his teachers in Egypt. "In the school that I went to in Cairo, corporal punishment [spanking] was part of the school life. We were even hit with a ruler for spelling mistakes." Raffi was delighted that the Canadian teachers didn't use physical punishment.

Learning English was not very difficult for Raffi because he was already used to learning new words in other languages. He was also good at grammar, the rules about forming sentences correctly. Raffi was ahead of his class in arithmetic, too, since he already knew how to do long division and multiplication.

Raffi remembers spending hours and hours drawing maps in school. "We used to have to draw maps in geography. We would get colored pencils and shave color shavings from the pencil. With a piece of cotton, we smudged the color on the paper and filled in the different countries."

Raffi's skill in drawing won him a chance to take free art classes, beginning in the sixth grade. For the next few years, Raffi spent Saturday mornings at the Toronto Art Gallery (now known as the Art Gallery of Ontario). There he studied drawing as well as watercolor and oil painting.

Art and schoolwork did not take up all of Raffi's time as he was growing up. He was also interested in ice hockey and baseball. His first hero was Frank Mahovlich, who played left wing for the Toronto Maple Leafs hockey team. Hank Aaron was his favorite baseball player.

Gradually, Raffi's interest turned to music. He spent time outside of school singing in Toronto's Armenian church choir with his father. "That was my first experience in singing and in trying to sing in tune," he says. In school, Raffi's sixth grade teacher, Mr. Horton, introduced him to folk music. One of Mr. Horton's friends played a twelve-string guitar for the class and sang, "Swing Low, Sweet Chariot." Raffi loved both the song and the full sound of the guitar.

In high school, Raffi heard several folksingers during school assemblies. He also began to listen to the records of folk performers such as Bob Dylan, Joan Baez, and Pete Seeger. He liked their songs about caring for the world and its people.

When he was sixteen, Raffi got his first guitar and taught himself to play several songs by the Beatles. "I had a friend who used to play the trumpet," Raffi remembers. "I played chords and he played the melody. At first, I didn't sing along. I remember the very first time I tried to sing and play the guitar at the same time. I thought, 'Oh, this is impossible.' I honestly thought that it was something that couldn't be done."

Raffi and his friends loved singing harmonies and teaching each other new chords to songs by Gordon Lightfoot, Bob Dylan, and Peter, Paul, and Mary. Raffi's favorite songs were "Four Strong Winds," "Michael Row the Boat Ashore," and "Yellow Bird."

Raffi plays guitar at a family Christmas gathering.

All this practicing bothered Raffi's parents, who wanted to throw his guitar in the trash. They worried that Raffi would pay more attention to music than to his schoolwork.

Despite his parents' fears, Raffi graduated from high school and then went on to the University of

Toronto. He planned to become a high school history teacher.

Before long, though, Raffi discovered that he loved music too much to stay in college. He left the university to sing regularly in local coffeehouses, places where many people went to hear folk music. At the coffeehouses, Raffi worked hard to learn finger picking, a difficult guitar method. He also explored different kinds of folk songs: lullabies and funny songs, songs with wonderful lilting melodies, and songs that told of traditions of the past. These songs would become very important as he moved to a new stage of his career—singing for children.

Raffi visits his niece Kristen at her nursery school to help celebrate her third birthday.

2

Singable Songs

While he was singing in the coffeehouses, Raffi wrote "Thinking Only of You," a song for his former high school girlfriend, Debi Pike. He hadn't seen Debi for four years, so he invited her to listen to him perform—and she loved "her" song. They began dating again. After a few years, they were married.

Debi taught kindergarten while Raffi continued to perform folk music for adult audiences. Then in 1974, Debi's mother, Daphne Pike, asked Raffi to sing at her preschool. Raffi didn't know any children's songs, so he asked Debi what to sing for three- and four-year-olds. She wrote down the words to "Eensy Weensy Spider," "Baa, Baa, Black Sheep," and a few other songs.

Raffi entertains some schoolchildren with singable songs.

Raffi began performing occasionally in class-rooms. After he had sung several times at her pre-school, Daphne Pike suggested that he record an album for young people. She had searched for modern, high-quality children's recordings, but couldn't locate any.

Raffi and Debi bought every children's album they could find. They listened to them over and over again with friends Bonnie and Bert Simpson, who were teachers that Debi knew. Most of these albums had been recorded in the early 1950s, so they didn't have a modern sound. Some were really albums for adults, not children.

The four friends decided that Raffi should make an album especially for young people. He chose songs of interest to children ages three to seven and included several familiar pieces. But he also added new ones such as "Down by the Bay" and "Willoughby Wallaby Woo," a funny rhyming song about an elephant that sits on people.

Through his own record company, Troubadour Records, Raffi arranged for a loan of four thousand dollars. In 1976, *Singable Songs for the Very Young* was recorded with the aid of Raffi's friend and fellow musician, Ken Whiteley. Ken said they hoped that they would eventually sell ten to fifteen thousand copies of the album.

The first two thousand were gone in just two months, with Raffi personally delivering them to children's bookstores out of the back of his station wagon. In four months, so many copies sold that he had to hire a local company to deliver the records.

"All of a sudden," Raffi says, "everybody wanted me for concerts." Still, Raffi wasn't sure he wanted to be a children's entertainer, even though a thousand children and their parents would come to an afternoon concert. At the same hall in the evening, fewer than fifty people would show up for his concert for adults.

Raffi kept up his dual career for two years. After recording *More Singable Songs*, he decided that he didn't have to be concerned about giving up adult folksinging. Raffi credits Debi and his former manager, Glenn Sernyk, with convincing him of the value of performing just for children. Raffi explains, "I realized that something rare was happening. I saw what a wonderful part I could play in a young child's life, and I realized that not everyone could entertain children."

Glenn worked hard to schedule more and more children's concerts for Raffi and planned tours to many cities. For concerts in larger auditoriums, Glenn arranged for Ken Whiteley to play and sing with Raffi onstage.

Ken continued to work with Raffi in the studio. In 1979, Ken helped Raffi record his third album, *The Corner Grocery Store.*

That same year, during a visit to Vancouver, British Columbia, Raffi and Debi saw beluga whales. These beautiful, playful mammals brought back memories of adult folk songs Raffi had sung about looking after the earth's creatures. Together, Debi and Raffi wrote "Baby Beluga," which tells of a baby whale swimming wild and free in the ocean. They knew children would enjoy the song because children love babies. But Debi and Raffi also used the song to tell about their love of the beautiful beluga.

"Baby Beluga" became the title song of a very different kind of children's album. Raffi decided to take a chance and include other songs that explored human feelings and needs such as "All I Really Need" and "Thanks A Lot."

The album quickly became just as popular as Raffi's earlier recordings, selling more than fifty thousand copies in Canada. His fans clearly liked Raffi's experiment in exploring his personal feelings through his songs.

Raffi's next recording, *Rise and Shine,* includes

"many songs about feeling good about yourself," according to Bert Simpson. For instance, the title song urges kids to rise each day, ready to do their best. *Raffi's Christmas Album*, which came out in 1983, focuses on the warm feelings of this special time of year.

His next album, *One Light, One Sun*, explores Raffi's belief that "we are all part of one global human family." It contains many songs about the experiences people share, no matter where they live. Raffi noticed that in most of the drawings of the outdoors that children sent him, the sun was pictured. He used the album's title song to remind everyone that the same sun shines over us all, "one light warming everyone."

Raffi's appreciation of the natural world is explored in *Everything Grows*. The 1987 album gets its name from a joyful song Raffi wrote with Debi about how all living creatures, whether they are plants,

Raffi's fans appreciate the care that goes into Raffi's projects.

animals, or people, are growing all the time.

Raffi treats his listeners to a mix of nonsense melodies, instrumentals (no singing), and pieces sung in foreign languages. Different musical styles and rhythms are used, played on a variety of instruments, including jaw harp, banjo, and trumpet.

Raffi's albums are all carefully planned and produced, so that "the finished music smiles at the listener." He doesn't rush through his work. *Everything Grows*, for example, took three months to record.

Raffi records and oversees the production of his albums himself in Toronto. When he is satisfied with the recording, he makes several master tapes of the album. Other companies, such as A&M Records, will transfer the music from the master tapes to records, cassette tapes, and compact discs (high-quality miniature records).

The many people who listened to Raffi's music appreciated the care and pride he took in his work. With the release of each new album, his popularity grew. Yet Raffi's success was not achieved alone. It took the help and support of many people, including his wife, his friends, and his fans.

Raffi and Debi.

3

A Musical Team

From the beginning, Raffi's wife Debi played an important part in his career as a young people's performer. Drawing on her background as a kindergarten and first grade teacher, she encouraged Raffi to sing old favorites, such as "I've Been Working on the Railroad," and songs about real life activities, such as brushing teeth and going on picnics. Her advice has been so helpful that Raffi says, "Debi has been my number one teacher in opening my eyes to the world of children."

When Raffi first started Troubadour Records, the company was headquartered in Raffi and Debi's dining room. It became a warehouse, or storage center, lined with metal shelves full of records and tapes.

Stacks of music and plans for concerts and albums covered the dining room table.

Now the headquarters of Troubadour Records is an office in a suburb of Toronto. Raffi plans his concerts and albums there, but does his recording in a variety of Toronto studios. Raffi's albums and tapes are now kept in the warehouses of companies such as A&M Records, which ship them out to stores.

Troubadour is not large when compared with other record companies. Only seven people work there, including Raffi. But the company is unusual because all the employees work together on each project.

Bert and Bonnie Simpson are an important part of Troubadour Records and have become Raffi's close friends. Whenever he talks about his career plans, Raffi says "we" to include Debi, Bonnie, and

Raffi and Bonnie and Bert Simpson display an award for Singable Songs for the Very Young.

Bert. They work together as a team, planning albums and concerts and writing songs such as "Let's Make Some Noise," "Peanut Butter Sandwich," and "The Sharing Song."

Raffi also gives credit for much of his success to Ken Whiteley. Ken is known throughout Canada for the many kinds of music he performs, including gospel, blues, and folk music. When he accompanied Raffi in concert, Ken was surrounded onstage by several instruments, including guitar, banjo, fiddle, accordion, and even a grand piano. Ken also helped Raffi oversee the recording of his first seven albums. His advice helped Raffi plan a variety of music for his albums and concerts.

Ken was one of the first members of Raffi's Rise and Shine Band, along with Dennis Pendrith, who plays bass guitar, and Bucky Berger, who plays the drums. Sometimes the membership of the band changes. Ken Whiteley decided to tour less after he and his wife had a baby. In 1987, two new members joined Dennis and Bucky. Mitchell Lewis plays a variety of stringed instruments, and Nancy Walker plays piano and electronic keyboards.

For albums, additional musicians are added.

Raffi and the Rise and Shine Band: (left to right) Dennis Pendrith, Bucky Berger, Raffi, Nancy Walker, and Mitchell Lewis.

Toronto, where Troubadour Records is based, is a major Canadian recording center, so well-known musicians are often available to play on a Raffi recording.

Many of Raffi's albums include children singing along, just as they would during a concert. The children who sang on the first two albums were children whom Raffi knew, such as Bert and Bonnie Simpson's sons, Justin and Joel. For later albums, Raffi and Debi asked music teacher Catherine Ambrose to help select young singers.

For each album, Catherine chooses five or six enthusiastic children who can sing in tune. During the recording session, the children listen through headphones to the melody Raffi has already recorded. As they sing along, each of their voices is recorded on a separate tape. A recording engineer can copy the tapes to make it sound as if two or even three times the number of children are singing.

During the recording session, the children learn a lot about making an album, since their part of the taping takes four to six hours of work. Catherine says, "They find out recording artists don't just go to the studio, sing their songs once, and go home. It is hard work, but enjoyable and rewarding."

Bonnie Simpson notes that Raffi credits anyone who helps him, and his backup singers are not forgotten. Raffi gives each child an autographed copy of the album he or she helped make. He presented autographed gold records to Debi's former school because so many of the students there have been recorded on his albums.

Making albums that children enjoy is only part of Raffi's career. He also continues to give concerts for children all over North America. And his concerts alone have earned Raffi many fans, young and old alike.

4
Show Time

As Raffi made albums and performed throughout North America, more and more people began to hear about his concerts. People who enjoyed Raffi's music told their friends. Children's bookstores sponsored his concerts by displaying posters and selling tickets. Eventually his performances were so popular that ticket lines formed three hours before show time. The audience sizes grew, too, although Raffi has had to limit their numbers so that everyone can be close enough to see and hear him.

To encourage families to enjoy the shows together, Raffi and Debi decided against asking the children to come down and sit in front of the stage. They found that in a darkened auditorium, some young

Raffi in concert.

children became fearful when separated from their parents. Children also missed the chance to sing along with their families.

When performing, Raffi seems to talk directly to each person in the audience. He is relaxed and natural. He wears comfortable, casual clothing and no stage makeup. Raffi gives the feeling that each concert takes place in a cozy family living room.

If he makes a mistake during the show, Raffi hopes children will learn from the way he handles it. Once, when he started to play a song in the wrong key, he just stopped and began again, playing the right notes.

Raffi tries to get his audience actively involved in his performance. He asks questions and lets children answer. When Raffi challenges the audience to make the sound of a kazoo, fans of all ages "play" along. During "Let's Do the Numbers Rumba," he

Raffi sings "Mr. Sun" for concert goers.

encourages dancing in the aisles. Later, he invites everyone to take a deep breath and relax in their seats for the quiet song, "Like Me and You."

Much care is taken to make Raffi's touring shows enjoyable. Since many fans are coming to their first concert ever, Raffi wants to make sure the sound, lighting, and music are well done. He uses his own risers (stage platforms) and modern, high-quality lighting and sound equipment.

His own crew of stagehands and technicians brings the equipment to each concert in a large moving van. They also bring plenty of spare parts, such as extra batteries for Raffi's cordless microphone. The crew begins setting up the equipment and lights five or six hours before a concert is scheduled to begin.

Three hours before concert time, Raffi, Debi, and the band arrive from their hotel. On long concert tours, they sometimes drive from city to city in a special rented bus, large enough for the band and their instruments. In the back is a desk, and a sitting room where Raffi rests on long trips.

About two and a half hours before each show begins, Raffi checks the sound system. He and the band play the beginning of several songs to be sure each instrument and singer is heard at the correct volume. The sound technician makes any necessary changes.

Another pre-concert check is testing the bubble machine, which fills the air with silky bubbles when Raffi sings "Bathtime." The first time he used it, it bubbled too well—Raffi nearly swallowed some of the bubbles. Now one of his stagehands carefully mixes a special bubble solution from ordinary dishwashing liquid.

Before the concert, Raffi relaxes in a dressing room backstage. He checks the list of songs for that day's show. Raffi prepares for the show by warming up—tuning his guitar, strumming chords, and singing for about ten minutes. To soothe his throat, he sips herbal tea or cool water. Raffi might also have a snack, such as a toasted bagel with cream cheese, especially when he has two concerts on the same day.

Debi is very busy before and during concerts. Long before the first performance of each tour, she helps Raffi choose his songs and the order in which they will be performed. She keeps track of Raffi's travel and concert schedules, so that he is free to concentrate on his music. She is in charge of Raffi's wardrobe (his onstage clothes) and also helps the crew members with their work. She carries a walkie-talkie so Raffi's tour manager can call her about problems that may occur anywhere in the theater.

Each concert lasts forty-five minutes to an hour. When the performance ends, the audience applauds

Raffi meets with fans after a concert.

until Raffi returns to the stage for an encore (short additional performance). "You didn't go home, did you?" he jokes. After the encore and much applause, the audience leaves the auditorium, many still happily singing their favorite songs.

An admirer personally delivers a fan letter to Raffi.

5

Songs to Read

Raffi has been widely recognized as one of the leaders of the children's recording business. He has already sold more than three million recordings. *One Light, One Sun* was the first album by a children's performer to be recorded on compact disc. It was so popular that the first pressing sold out in four days.

As a leader in children's music, Raffi has earned many honors. In 1983, he was appointed a member of the Order of Canada, the country's highest non-military award. Raffi is one of the youngest people ever to receive this honor. The American recording industry also honored Raffi by nominating *Everything Grows* for a Grammy for the best children's recording of 1988.

Despite these honors and the attention they have drawn, Raffi never loses sight of the direction he wants his career to follow. Because of his appeal to children throughout North America, Raffi is often asked to make commercials or lend his name to such products as breakfast cereals or jazzy wrist watches. He turns down such offers. "I don't believe in giving my name and likeness to commercial products. My music is important in and of itself without being tied to television advertising. I'm here to make music that I feel good about and that makes people feel good and brings them together."

Raffi has also received several requests to put together a weekly children's television series, but he hasn't accepted these requests. He would rather have children play with their friends than constantly watch television. As "doers, not viewers," they learn best through playing and imagining. By spending

Raffi receives the Order of Canada medal.   49

hours in front of a television screen, they are watching what someone else has created instead of using their own imaginations.

Still, Raffi believes that television can be a wonderful tool when it's wisely used. "After all," he laughs, "I've been known to watch it myself!" Raffi decided to produce a quality program for children to watch and planned to videotape one of his concerts. The film would provide an opportunity for children to sing along and take part in what they were watching.

Called *A Young Children's Concert with Raffi*, the videocassette sold thousands of copies and was shown on the Disney Channel. Since he can't perform in every city, Raffi is glad the video gives everyone a chance to see a concert. And children who have been to a Raffi concert enjoy reliving the experience.

An imaginative girl dressed like Raffi for Halloween.   51

Raffi waited four years before starting work on another concert video. He didn't want to film another video just because the first one was successful. He decided to include his Rise and Shine Band, so that children will have the chance to see and hear the band play many different musical instruments while Raffi sings.

Families who enjoy Raffi's albums and videocassettes can also enjoy his music through his books. *The Raffi Singable Songbook* and *The Second Raffi Songbook* include the words and printed sheet music to the songs on Raffi's first six albums. He encourages family singalongs by giving tips to beginning guitar and piano players to help them learn to play his songs. *The Raffi Christmas Treasury* includes Christmas stories and pictures plus the words and music to the many holiday songs on *Raffi's Christmas Album*. In 1987, Crown Publishers asked Raffi to make his most familiar songs into individual picture books, called *Raffi Songs to Read*™. He was delighted, because "the songs-to-read idea was one that Debi, Bonnie, and Bert had talked about for quite a while." *Raffi Songs to Read*™ colorfully illustrate the words to favorite Raffi songs, such as "Shake My Sillies Out." The melody to each song is noted in the back.

Bert Simpson says that a "song to read" is a natural bridge between singing and reading. It shows children the words to songs they can already sing. The beginning reader can follow along as the book is read. Soon, the reader matches the words heard with the words on the printed page.

Whenever Raffi talks about his books or his music, he is very enthusiastic. His work fills him with joy. Raffi says that, as a youngster, "I couldn't have dreamed the work that I have now! I couldn't have imagined it!"

Raffi enjoys working, and playing, with children.

6

"Children Are My Life's Work"

Fame hasn't changed Raffi. Bookstore owners who meet him say he is just as friendly in person as he is on stage. He takes time for thoughtful actions. Once he sang "Happy Birthday" to a young girl who came to a concert in Denver. Her mother had written to tell Raffi that the concert was her birthday present.

Raffi receives mail from fans both young and old. "What children have to say to Raffi is very important," says Bonnie Simpson, who helps him answer his mail. "He loves to read what they think of his songs and is touched that children take the time to write to him." Children often invite Raffi to their birthday parties or ask him to visit their schools. However, his busy schedule makes that impossible.

Raffi tries to grant the requests of groups that help others. He has donated a favorite recipe for a boys' club cookbook and has given gifts for many auctions and telethons that raise money to aid the sick and the needy. Another important cause that Raffi supports is Pollution Probe, a Canadian group working to keep the air and water clean.

Whenever Raffi has "time off," he enjoys cheering for the Toronto Blue Jays baseball team. He likes to play with his dog Bundles, and goes bowling with Debi, Bonnie, and Bert. They wrote "The Bowling Song" about the fun they have together.

Raffi also spends a lot of free time reading. "I can't do without it!" he says. Much of his reading is about how children grow and develop. He, Debi, Bert, and Bonnie spend many hours discussing what they have read and deciding how to apply it to their work with children.

What children have to say about his songs is important to Raffi.

From his reading and his experiences growing up, Raffi knows childhood can sometimes be a confusing and frightening time. He remembers being teased about his name as a youngster, but now he's glad it is so unusual. Raffi hopes his music will help children enjoy whatever is special about themselves.

Raffi and his family: (left to right) Lucy (seated), Onnig, Raffi, Ann, and Artin.

Raffi says, "Children are my life's work." Even though he and Debi have none of their own, they have touched millions of children through music. They both encourage adults to pay attention to a child's unique view of the world. When a child asks, "How did you get out of your record, Raffi?" it is not a silly question. The child is truly seeking information. Yet, too often, Raffi says, grown-ups make fun of children for asking such questions, because they don't try to see things from the child's point of view.

Those who know Raffi have high praise for his work. "Raffi's songs explore the child's everyday world and yet also help the child reach beyond, to the world around us," explains Catherine Ambrose. Eda LeShan, known for her many books about children and families, says that Raffi treats each child as a special treasure. "He allows children to be children.

He's in no hurry. He wants to have fun with children, and children know immediately how much he cares about them." She calls Raffi a true troubadour, or poet-musician, for children and their needs.

Whatever Raffi chooses to do in the future, his work will continue to please children and their families. His music reminds us to share our love with all the world's people and to appreciate every living thing. In Raffi's own words, "Making music is an expression of joy in living. To me, that's what singing together is all about."

Raffi's Recordings and Books

Raffi's Recordings

Singable Songs for the Very Young, 1976
More Singable Songs, 1977
The Corner Grocery Store, 1979
Baby Beluga, 1980
Rise and Shine, 1982
Raffi's Christmas Album, 1983
One Light, One Sun, 1985
Everything Grows, 1987

Videocassettes:
A Young Children's Concert with Raffi, 1984
Raffi In Concert with the Rise and Shine Band, 1988

Raffi's Books

The Raffi Singable Songbook, 1987
The Second Raffi Songbook, 1987
Down by the Bay, 1987
Illustrated by Nadine Bernard Westcott
Shake My Sillies Out, 1987
Illustrated by David Allender
One Light, One Sun, 1988
Illustrated by Eugenie Fernandes
The Wheels on the Bus, 1988
Illustrated by Sylvie Kantorovitz Wickstrom
The Raffi Christmas Treasury, 1988
Illustrated by Nadine Bernard Westcott

Index

About the Author

A freelance writer with a strong interest in children and family
life, Karen Spies has long been a Raffi fan and admirer. For
this book, she interviewed Raffi and his associates, and
attended one of his concerts to get a firsthand view of his
audience.

Spies has taught preschool through sixth grade classes, and
has served as an elementary school vice-principal. Her books
include *Denver*, a Downtown America book, and *Family
Activities for the Christmas Season*. She has also written for
Highlights, Jack and Jill, Children's Digest, and *Child Life*.
Currently, she conducts writing workshops for children's
authors as well as workshops for young writers. She lives with
her husband and two children in Littleton, Colorado.